frican Americans
ilitary

By Jessica Morrison

www.av2books.com

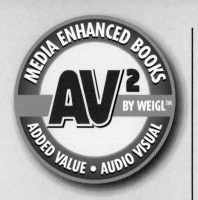

Go to **www.av2books.com**, and enter this book's unique code.

BOOK CODE

M 9 6 3 6 6 5

AV² by Weigl brings you media enhanced books that support active learning.

AV² provides enriched content that supplements and complements this boo Weigl's AV² books strive to create inspired learning and engage young min in a total learning experience.

Your AV² Media Enhanced books come alive with...

Audio
Listen to sections of the book read aloud.

Video
Watch informative video clips.

Embedded Weblinks
Gain additional information for research.

Try This!
Complete activities and hands-on experiments.

Key Words
Study vocabulary, and complete a matching word activity.

Quizzes
Test your knowledge.

Slide Show
View images and captions, and prepare a presentation.

... and much, much more

Published by AV² by Weigl
350 5th Avenue, 59th Floor
New York, NY 10118

Website: www.weigl.com   www.av2books.com

Library of Congress Cataloging-in-Publication Data

Morrison, Jessica.
 Military / Jessica Morrison.
    p. cm. -- (Great African Americans)
Includes index.
 ISBN 978-1-61690-661-0 (hardcover : alk. paper) -- ISBN 978-1-61690-665-8 (softcover : alk. paper)
1. African American soldiers--History--Juvenile literature. 2. United States--Armed Forces--African Americans--History--Juvenile literature. I. Title.
 E185.63.M68 2011
 355.0092--dc22
                          2010050183

Printed in the United States of America in North Mankato, Minnesota
1 2 3 4 5 6 7 8 9 0 15 14 13 12 11

062011
WEP290411

Weigl acknowledges Getty Images as its primary image supplier for this title.

Every reasonable effort has been made to trace ownership and to obtain permission to reprint copyright material. The publishers would be pleased to have any errors or omissions brought to their attention so that they may be corrected in subsequent printings.

Senior Editor: Heather Kissock
Art Director: Terry Paulhus

USN-702

Contents

A Call to Arms

For more than 200 years, every war in U.S. history has involved African American soldiers. Their contributions have helped to build and defend the nation. African Americans, however, have not always been allowed to defend their home alongside other soldiers. Racial **discrimination**, as well as social customs and practices, created tensions that were evident during times of both war and peace. Before the Civil War, when slavery was legal, African Americans were not even officially recognized as people and were not given the same status or rights as other Americans. They did not have the right to vote or to own property, nor did they have basic personal freedom.

Despite this, over the years, African Americans have fought bravely for their country, many dying in battle and making huge sacrifices. Their many accomplishments in the military were not always given the recognition they deserved, and they were not always given the respect afforded other soldiers. Yet while fighting for their country, they overcame obstacles in their path to take their rightful place, not only in the military but in U.S. society as well.

African American soldiers throughout U.S. history, including those who saw action during World War I, were proud to serve their country.

The American Revolution

The American Revolution was a turning point in the history of the United States. Beginning in the 1760s, many Americans living in the British colonies were unhappy. They believed that they were being taxed unfairly, and they wanted to be independent of Great Britain. African Americans, most of whom were slaves in both the North and the South, were very much a part of the conflict.

War broke out in 1775. That year, George Washington, the commander of the **Continental Army**, issued an order stating that African Americans could not be **recruited** to serve in the army. African Americans were also not allowed to **enlist** in many local **militias**. Many colonists feared that African Americans might revolt if they were given arms, and these people wanted to keep weapons out of the hands of slaves.

African Americans joined others in America to protest British rule in the years before the American Revolution.

On the Side of the British

African Americans were divided about whether to support the colonists or the British. To get their support, some British leaders in America promised the slaves that they would be given their freedom if they sided with Great Britain. In late 1775, John Murray, who was the Earl of Dunmore and the British royal governor of Virginia, began to enlist African American soldiers. Nearly 300 African Americans joined what became known as Lord Dunmore's "Ethiopian **Regiment**." Overall, at least 20,000 African Americans served on the British side.

George Washington came to believe that slavery was wrong. He arranged for his slaves to be freed after he and his wife died.

New Colonial Attitude

When the colonial leaders realized that they might be defeated by the British, they began to rethink their strategy about enlisting African Americans. General Washington eventually decided to lift his ban, and 8,000 to 10,000 African Americans ultimately fought on the colonial side. Some were slaves, while others were free men. Many of the African Americans were offered money, earning 10 dollars to enlist. Also, able-bodied men of European descent were **exempt** from enlisting if they could produce a suitable substitute, and African Americans often stood in for them. Most African Americans were eager to serve, believing that they might gain their freedom when the fighting ended.

TECHNOLOGY LINK

To find out more about African Americans during the American Revolution, visit **http://www.pbs.org/wgbh/aia/part2/title.html**.

Gallant Soldiers, Unfair Treatment

Despite being granted the right to join the military, African Americans during the American Revolution were often treated unfairly. They were usually given jobs as laborers rather than as fighting soldiers.

Yet many African Americans, such as Salem Poor, showed great bravery. Poor had been born into slavery in 1748, but he bought his freedom in 1769. In 1775, he and his militia unit were stationed opposite British troops in Boston, Massachusetts. On June 17, 1775, at the Battle of Bunker Hill, Poor became one of the biggest heroes of the Revolution. He **mortally wounded** an important British officer, Lieutenant Colonel James Abercrombie. Fourteen American officers praised Poor's heroism and asked the General Court of Massachusetts to recognize his performance. In 1975, Poor was honored with a postage stamp citing him as a "gallant soldier."

After the Revolution

When the American Revolution ended in 1783, the United States gained its freedom. African Americans hoped their contributions would gain them equality, but they were often disappointed. About 0 percent of the African Americans who fought were freed from slavery, but many African Americans had trouble receiving their **pensions**. In addition, slave owners refused to grant freedom to the slaves who fought as substitutes in their place.

In 1790, there were almost 700,000 slaves in the United States.

Quick Facts

African Americans from all 13 colonies fought for independence from Great Britain.

While there were several regiments made up of just African Americans during the Revolution, notably those from Rhode Island and Massachusetts, most African Americans served in **integrated** units.

The New Nation

African Americans had done their part during the American Revolution. They were disappointed, however, in hoping that they would be free in the new nation. Slavery continued to exist. In 1807, 20 years after the U.S. Constitution was written, President Thomas Jefferson signed a bill that made it illegal to import slaves into the United States. Many Americans, however, continued to own and sell slaves.

African Americans, including veterans of the American Revolution, were denied a place in state militias set up to defend the new nation in times of emergency. The wording of the Militia Act of 1792, passed by the U.S. Congress, excluded African Americans. The act called for "each

In the 1800s, slaves were routinely bought and sold in the southern states. Families were often split apart.

African Americans fought bravely in the Battle of New Orleans, which was the last major battle of the War of 1812.

...d every able-bodied white male ...tizen" to enroll.

...he War of 1812

...1811, a number of U.S. ships ...ere fired upon by British ships. ...ch incidents caused President ...mes Madison to ask Congress for ...declaration of war, and the War ...1812 officially began in June of ...at year. Since the U.S. Army had ...ecome very small, there was a shortage of U.S. soldiers. As a result, in 1813, Congress passed a law allowing the enlistment of "persons of color." Many African Americans subsequently enlisted.

During the War of 1812, many African Americans served in the U.S. Navy, where they had always been allowed to enlist. They made up an estimated 10 percent of sailors serving on Navy ships in the Great Lakes region.

Attitudes Toward African American Sailors

Not all naval commanders were happy to have African American sailors on board their ships. The naval hero Oliver Hazard Perry was one of those commanders. He wrote to his superior, Commodore Isaac Chauncey, to complain. Chauncey stood up for the African American sailors. "I regret that you are not pleased with the men sent you, . . . " Chauncey wrote. "I have yet to learn that the color of the skin, or cut and trimmings of the coat, can affect a man's qualifications or usefulness. I have nearly 50 blacks on board of this ship, and many of them are among my best men."

Victory in the War of 1812

Oliver Hazard Perry was in command of the naval forces when the U.S. Navy won an important victory at the Battle of Lake Erie, on September 10, 1813. The victory ensured that Americans controlled the Great Lakes. About one-quarter of the sailors involved were African American. The United States defeated the British at Lake Erie largely because of the participation of the African Americans. Perry had once criticized African American

Sailor Cyrus Tiffany is said to have saved Oliver Hazard Perry's life by shielding the commodore's body when the British began firing on their ship.

The First and Second Battalions of Free Men of Color, made up of 600 African Americans, played important roles in the Battle of New Orleans.

ilors, but he changed his opinion f these men, noting their bravery. They seemed to be absolutely nsensible to danger," Perry said.

Unfit to Associate"

t the end of 1814, the United tates and Great Britain reached an greement to end the war. Congress assed a measure in 1815 that reated an army of 10,000 men, but o African Americans were recruited. War Department memorandum sued that year described African mericans as "unfit to associate with ne American soldier."

In the 1820s, African Americans ere prohibited from serving in

the Army or in state militias. Then, in the 1830s, the Navy imposed a **quota** to keep the number of African Americans under 5 percent of the total number of sailors.

Quick Facts

Most African Americans who served during the War of 1812 were subjected to the same discrimination they endured during peacetime.

Many units included men of different races, but African Americans were kept away from other soldiers and told to keep to themselves.

A Nation Divided

In the 1850s, tensions increased between the North and South in the United States. The economy in the North was based on **industrialization**. New factories had been built, bringing wealth to the region. In addition, since the industrial economy made use of machinery to produce goods, northerners did not need to rely on slaves. Soon, many northerners were questioning whether anyone should have slaves, and many northern states completely abolished slavery. Southerners, whose economy was agricultural, did not want to end slavery. Land owners needed slaves to grow crops such as tobacco and cotton on their large farms, called plantations. Southerners also feared that without slavery, their region would get poorer, leaving them with less power than the North. Even southerners who did not own slaves supported the slave system.

The Civil War Begins

In November 1860, Abraham Lincoln was elected president. He opposed slavery but did not set out to abolish it. Instead, he wanted to prevent slavery from being extended into new U.S. territories in the West. Lincoln's election worried and angered southerners who felt that their way of life was threatened. In the months after Lincoln's election, southern states began to secede, or break away, from the rest of the United States to form their own country, called the Confederate States of America.

Lincoln was **inaugurated** in March 1861. The Civil War began the next month, when Confederate troops fired on Fort Sumter in South Carolina. Lincoln called for 75,000 volunteers to fight for the Union, as the North was called. He did not, however, permit the recruiting of African Americans for the Union Army, and those who tried to enlist were rejected. When the Civil War began, Lincoln viewed it as a conflict to maintain and preserve the Union. He insisted that the war was not about slavery and the rights of African Americans.

Confederate forces captured Fort Sumter, a government fort in the harbor of Charleston, South Carolina, after 34 hours of fighting.

A Fight to End Slavery

African Americans did not see the Civil War as a battle to preserve the Union. To African Americans, it was a battle to end slavery. As a result, even though the North did not seek out African Americans, many slaves escaped from the South and volunteered to serve with the Union Army. In 1861 and 1862, Congress passed laws stating that fugitive slaves did not have to be returned to their owners. Congress also allowed the enlistment of African Americans, but Lincoln was reluctant to act on this. Nevertheless, regiments of African American volunteers were organized in various places, including areas in the South that had fallen to the Union.

On the Confederate side, African Americans were used during the Civil War for labor and other tasks. Southerners did not want to provide African Americans with guns or have them serve as combat troops.

Recruiting posters were used to urge African Americans to join the Union Army.

COME AND JOIN US BROTHERS.

PUBLISHED BY THE SUPERVISORY COMMITTEE FOR RECRUITING COLORED REGIMENTS

The Emancipation Proclamation

On January 1, 1863, President Lincoln's **Emancipation Proclamation** went into effect. This document declared "that all persons held as slaves" within the Confederate states "are, and henceforward shall be free." This meant that many former slaves and other African Americans could now enter and serve in the Union military.

Some African Americans served as combat troops, while others played different roles. Many were assigned to move equipment or dig ditches. Some worked in hospitals and as chaplains. Others worked as spies for the Union Army. Despite their contributions, though, African Americans faced **prejudice** and discrimination. At first, many who fought were given arms that were not as good as those provided to other soldiers. African Americans also received lower pay than other troops. In time, conditions improved and African Americans were given better pay. In addition, by the time the war ended, about 100 African Americans had been named officers. These people were in positions of authority and often in command of other men.

Frederick Douglass

Frederick Douglass was born a slave in 1817 in Maryland. When he was 21, he escaped and went to New York. He became a leader of the **abolitionist movement**. Douglass believed that all people should have equal rights, including African Americans, American Indians, women, and recent immigrants. He was known as a forward-thinking man and **eloquent** speaker. He wrote, "I would unite with anybody to do right and with nobody to do wrong."

During the early stages of the Civil War, Douglass urged President Lincoln to free slaves who were willing to fight for the Union. He also urged the military to arm African Americans, something that military leaders were hesitant to do at first. Douglass served a very important role in recruiting African Americans to the 54th Massachusetts **Infantry** Regiment, which was the first regiment of African American soldiers. His own sons, Charles and Lewis, enlisted in the regiment. Until his death in 1895, Douglass was a face for equality.

African Americans in the Civil War

Anumber of African American regiments were formed during the Civil War. Most were led by officers of European heritage. The best-known was the 54th Massachusetts Infantry Regiment, commanded by Colonel Robert Gould Shaw, who was not African American and was the son of well-known abolitionists from Boston. The regiment served bravely in an attack on Fort Wagner, South Carolina, in July 1863. Half the soldiers in the regiment, including Colonel Shaw, were killed during the battle.

The Fort Pillow Massacre

A hard-fought battle took place in April 1864 at Fort Pillow, Tennessee. The fort was held by 600 Union troops, half of them former slaves. Approximately 3,000 Confederates attacked the fort. Almost two-thirds of the African American soldiers were killed by the Confederates, many after they had surrendered.

Quick Facts

During the Civil War, some 180,000 African Americans served in combat units. About 90,000 of them were from the South.

African Americans made up approximately 10 percent of the Union Army.

More than 29,000 African Americans served as sailors in the Union Navy.

An estimated 37,000 African Americans were killed during the Civil War. More than 30,000 others were wounded.

Twenty-five African Americans were awarded the Congressional **Medal of Honor**.

The Civil War Ends

The Civil War ended in 1865 with the surrender of the Confederacy. African American soldiers accounted for 10 percent of all Union casualties. They played an important part in the Union's victory. During the war, African Americans had earned the right to live as free men. In December 1865, the Thirteenth Amendment to the U.S. Constitution, abolishing slavery throughout the United States, was approved.

African Americans sometimes served as a picket post. This was a small group of soldiers acting as guards to warn of the approach of the Confederates.

The Indian Wars

In 1866, Congress passed a law allowing African Americans to serve in the regular peacetime army. Soon, African American soldiers were called upon to fight American Indians in the West. The soldiers were needed in these Indian wars. After the Civil War, many American had moved west, where they hoped to settle. This brought them into conflict with the Indians living on the land. U.S. Army units were sent to intervene in these conflicts.

Buffalo Soldiers

Four new African American Army regiments were created. Two were **cavalry** regiments, the 9th and the 10th Cavalries, and two were infantry regiments, the 24th and 25th Regiments. They were made up mostly of former slaves and Civil War veterans. In 1867, the 9th and 10th Cavalries were sent out West. American Indians called the African Americans "Buffalo Soldiers," possibl because their hair was thought to look similar to buffalo manes.

The Buffalo Soldiers often had to guide their horses down steep mountain passes. Their assignments took them to North and South Dakota, Texas, Arizona, and other areas.

Conditions in the West

The West was a hostile place for the Buffalo Soldiers. Often, other soldiers made them camp outside the forts. They endured harsh conditions, such as extreme heat in the summer and cold in the winter. Still, the Buffalo Soldiers were loyal and successful in their military assignments. They fought hundreds of battles against different Indian troups. In 1867, in a two-day battle near Fort Leavenworth, Kansas, 90 members of the 10th Cavalry defeated 00 Cheyenne. In 1885 and 1886, the 10th Cavalry fought against Geronimo, the Apache chief, who eventually surrendered to them.

The Buffalo Soldiers were often given horses that had been rejected by other cavalry troops. They were also given secondhand equipment.

Henry O. Flipper

Henry O. Flipper was born a slave in Georgia in 1856. In 1877, he became the first African American to graduate from the U.S. Military Academy at West Point. He became a lieutenant in the 10th Cavalry and was the first African American officer to command troops. Although Flipper served his regiment well in the Indian wars, like other African American soldiers, he encountered discrimination on a regular basis. He was accused of **embezzlement** and was dishonorably discharged from the Army in 1881. Flipper went on to a successful career as an editor, miner, and **surveyor** in the Southwest. The Army finally cleared him of wrongdoing in 1976, 36 years after his death.

The Spanish-American War

The African American regiments that had fought in the Indian wars continued to serve and were among the soldiers who fought in the Spanish-American War in 1898. This conflict came about in part when the United States supported Cuba, which wanted independence from Spain. The African American regiments were sent to the southern United States for training, then on to fight in Cuba, which is located not far from Florida. Other African Americans were recruited because authorities mistakenly believed that they would be better able to resist different tropical diseases in Cuba because of their African heritage.

Notable Engagements

The African American regiments took part in some of the most important battles of the war, although they did not always receive the recognition they deserved. The Rough Riders were a volunteer regiment led by Theodore Roosevelt, who later became president. On three occasions, the African American regiments came to the Rough Riders' rescue. This occurred in the battles of Las Guásimas, El Caney, and San Juan Hill. The Rough Riders were grateful to the African American soldiers, as was Roosevelt. Later in his career, however, Roosevelt began to maintain that these soldiers had succeeded because they were led by men of European heritage.

The bravery of the African American cavalries did not go entirely unnoticed. Newspapers reported on their bravery and accomplishments, and six of the men earned the Medal of Honor.

enjamin O. Davis Sr.

ewer than 10 African Americans became commissioned officers between 1899 and 1948. Benjamin O. Davis Sr. was e of them. Born in Washington, D.C., in 77, Davis had wanted to be an officer ce childhood. He graduated from Howard iversity, where he was a member of the rican American unit of the National Guard. volunteered to fight in the Spanish-nerican War. In 1899, he enlisted as a ivate in the regular Army. He was regularly omoted, and in 1941, he became a igadier general, the first African American attain that rank. Davis died in 1970. His n, Benjamin O. Davis Jr., would follow him having a distinguished military career.

Quick Facts

The Spanish-American War was the most integrated war since the American Revolution. African American soldiers fought alongside other soldiers.

African American soldiers endured harsh racism and discrimination when they underwent training in Florida and Georgia prior to being sent to Cuba.

Following the war, African American regiments were sent to fight in the Philippines, where residents were rebelling against U.S. rule.

African American regiments made up 12 percent of the total forces involved in the invasion of Cuba.

World War I Begins

By the 20th century, African Americans had played a role in every war that had been fought in U.S. history. Despite this, when World War I began, the U.S. armed forces remained **segregated**. At first, many African Americans who tried to enlist were turned down at recruiting stations.

African Americans saw the war as an opportunity to show their loyalty and patriotism. They wanted to prove that they deserved equal treatment in U.S. society.

The Buffalo Soldier Division

The Army's four African American units still existed. In late 1917, the government created two new African American Army combat units, the 92nd and 93rd Divisions. The 92nd Division was nicknamed the Buffalo Soldier Division in order to gain support from African Americans. The division was not given proper training or leadership, and the men were not respected from the start by their commander, who was not African American. Still, its soldiers performed well in combat during the late stages of the war.

A total of 103 officers and 1,543 enlisted men in the 92nd Division

Certain recruiting posters during World War I were specifically aimed at African American men.

The Course of World War I

World War I began in Europe after the Archduke Franz Ferdinand of Austria was assassinated in June 1914. Within weeks, most of Europe was at war, but the United States remained **neutral** for almost three years. The United States finally entered the war in April 1917 on the side of the Allies, which included France and Great Britain, and against Germany, Austria-Hungary, and the other Central Powers.

...ied during the war, either in
...ction or from wounds or disease.
...ourteen African American officers
...nd 43 enlisted men received the
...istinguished Service Cross, which
...s a high military honor.

The Harlem Hellfighters

The 93rd Division was made up of
...our infantry regiments. The most
...amous was the 369th Infantry,
...hich hailed from New York. The
...en were known as the Harlem
...ellfighters, since Harlem was a
...eighborhood in New York where
...any African Americans lived.
...he men of the 369th Infantry were
...osted to France, where they fought
...n the front lines for 191 straight
...ays. This was longer than any other

U.S. unit. By the time the war ended,
the 369th Infantry had suffered
1,500 casualties.

The 369th Infantry, fighting in France, took part in some of the most important
actions against the Germans in World War I.

Heading Home

After World War I ended in November 1918, the Allies staged a grand victory parade in Paris, but African American troops were not allowed to take part. There were other snubs as well. African American soldiers had the job of loading coal into the battleship USS *Virginia*, which was to transport troops home. When they began to load their own gear, however, they were told by the captain that they could not come onboard because African Americans had never been allowed on his ship and none ever would be.

African American soldiers were also given the job of cleaning up after the war in Europe. For example, 9,000 African Americans were told to rebury all of the dead in American cemeteries built near the battlefields. It was difficult for many African American soldiers to deal with the inequality of treatment after the ordeals they had lived through. William Hewlett, an African American private, wrote in August 1919, "Why did black men die here in France 3,300 miles from their home? Was it to make democracy safe for the white people in America, with the black race left out?"

African American soldiers returning home found that little had changed and that hostility toward African Americans continued. They had served their country and expected to be greeted as heroes. Instead, they faced continuing discrimination and an increase in racial tension.

Many people did not think that African Americans could be good soldiers. The African American men who fought in World War I showed that this belief was wrong.

Victory Parade

In one instance, African American soldiers were welcomed back as heroes. In February 1919, the men of the 369th Infantry were given a homecoming parade up New York City's Fifth Avenue. The city also honored the troops with a special dinner. However, although many African American soldiers were honored by the French government, not one was awarded a Medal of Honor by his own country during World War I. In 1991, the medal was finally awarded, **posthumously**, to Corporal Freddie Stowers. In September 1918, while serving as a squad leader in the 371st Infantry, Stowers had led an assault on German lines, even after he was fatally wounded. He was the only African American World War I soldier to receive the medal.

Nearly 1 million people lined New York City's Fifth Avenue to welcome the 369th Infantry home. Children in Harlem were given the day off from school so they could attend the parade.

Limited Roles

Many commanders did not believe that African Americans could perform well in battle. As a result, the vast majority of African Americans in the Army did not see actual combat during World War I. Most were limited to jobs at military bases as laborers or stevedores, unloading cargo ships. They also delivered food and other supplies, built railway lines and warehouses, and prepared meals.

World War II Begins

On September 1, 1939, World War II broke out in Europe when Germany invaded Poland. As in World War I, the United States, whose military was still segregated, did not enter the war right away.

In 1939, there were only 3,640 African Americans in the U.S. Army. In the Navy, African Americans could serve only in the galleys, or kitchens, of ships. There were still no African Americans in the Marines or Air Corps.

Before and After Pearl Harbor
In September 1940, with entry into the war becoming a greater possibility, President Franklin D. Roosevelt signed into law the nation's first peacetime military draft. It required all men between the ages of 21 and 35 to register with their local draft boards. African Americans turned up in large numbers at their local offices to register. Many of them were turned away because the Army did not have enough

After the United States entered World War II, African Americans were sent to fight in Europe and the Pacific.

egregated facilities for training hem. By the end of 1940, only 539 frican Americans had been added o the Army. Then, on December 7, 941, Japan attacked the U.S. naval ase at Pearl Harbor, Hawaii. The Jnited States entered World War following the attack. The nation ought on the side of the Allies, such s Great Britain and France, and gainst the Axis, including Germany nd Japan. U.S. entry into the war ed to the enlistment of more

African Americans. By late 1942, almost 500,000 African Americans were in the Army. As in previous wars, they encountered segregation and discrimination.

TECHNOLOGY LINK

To find out more about World War II, visit **http://www.pbs. org/perilousfight/**.

Dorie Miller

oris Miller, called Dorie, was born in 1919 in Texas. He joined the Navy in 939 and was a cook's assistant n the battleship USS *West irginia*, which was stationed at earl Harbor. After the ship was orpedoed by the Japanese, Miller elped carry wounded sailors safety. Then, even though he ad never been trained to use machine gun, he manned one ntil orders came to abandon hip. For his actions, Miller ecame the first African American receive the Navy Cross, in May 942. He was killed in November 943 when his next ship was orpedoed by the Japanese and ınk in the Pacific Ocean.

"above and beyond the call of duty"

DORIE MILLER
Received the Navy Cross at Pearl Harbor, May 27, 1942

The Tuskegee Airmen

In the late 1930s, the United States began a pilot training program. African Americans were not allowed to fly military planes, but the training program was eventually opened to them. They were trained in a separate, all-black unit, the 99th Pursuit Squadron. Since their training site was at Tuskegee Army Air Field in Alabama, they became known as the Tuskegee Airmen.

At first, segregation occurred at the base. Signs read "For Colored Officers" and "For White Officers," and there were separate barracks, toilets, and drinking fountains for each group. Conditions improved when a new commander was appointed at the facility. He was understanding about the problems faced by the African American men, and he treated all people equally. With his help, the men of Tuskegee became fully trained combat pilots.

The Lonely Eagles to War

The Tuskegee Airmen preferred to call themselves the Lonely Eagles.

The Tuskegee Airmen were awarded the Medal of Honor in 2007, some 60 years after they completed their work in World War II.

Benjamin O. Davis Jr.

Like his father before him, Benjamin O. Davis Jr. was destined for a life in the military. He was born in Washington, D.C., in 1912 and graduated from the U.S. Military Academy at West Point in 1936. Davis was isolated during his four years at West Point. He roomed alone and ate alone and was shocked at the open discrimination he encountered. Taking command of an African American company in Georgia, Davis still encountered discrimination. Often, other officers refused to speak to him unless they had to. Davis transferred to the Army Air Corps, completed training as a military pilot, and became commander of the Tuskegee Airmen. Ultimately, in 1953, he became the first African American Air Force officer to achieve the rank of general. Davis died in 2002.

In April 1943, the Lonely Eagles of the 99th Pursuit Squadron were sent to fight in North Africa. They flew their first combat mission in June. In 1944, they joined the 332nd Fighter Group, made up of African American units. The 332nd Fighter Group, led by Benjamin O. Davis Jr., flew thousands of missions during World War II. They shot down 112 enemy planes and destroyed 150 more on the ground. They also destroyed almost 1,000 motor vehicles and railcars. Sixty-six of the Tuskegee Airmen were killed in action. An additional 32 were shot down and captured, becoming prisoners of war.

The Tuskegee Airmen were honored for their service in World War II. Among the many awards they earned were 150 Distinguished Flying Crosses and eight Purple Hearts, given to people who have been killed or wounded while serving.

TECHNOLOGY LINK

To find out more about the Tuskegee Airmen, visit http://www.nationalmuseum. af.mil/factsheets/ factsheet.asp?id=1356.

Coming Out Fighting

The Tuskegee Airmen were just one of the notable African American military units during World War II. The 761st Tank Battalion was the first African American armored combat unit. Their motto was "come out fighting," and they fought nonstop for six months in 30 major engagements, supporting the Army's advance into Germany. By the end of the war, they had lost half their men.

The Triple Nickels

The 555th Parachute Infantry Battalion, nicknamed the Triple Nickels, were the first African American paratroopers. They were sent on a special mission in 1945 called Operation Firefly. The Japanese had used balloons to send bombs across the Pacific. These bombs started forest fires in the Pacific Northwest. The men of the 555th became **smoke jumpers** defusing the bombs and putting out the fires.

The 6888th Central Postal Directory Battalion

Some 130 African American women served as Army nurses and Red Cross workers during World War II, while more than 4,000 enlisted in the Women's Army Corps, or WACs. Most did lower-level jobs, except for the 6888th Central Postal Directory Battalion, made up of

00 African American women. This nit was responsible for organizing nd routing letters sent to the U.S. oldiers serving in Europe. Major harity Adams, the battalion's ommander, was the first African merican officer in the WACs. The omen played a major role in eeping up the morale of the soldiers.

Continued Struggle . War and Home

uring World War II, the number f African Americans in the military ose to more than 900,000. Even the larines, which had once excluded frican Americans, now included iem. When the war ended in 1945 id African American soldiers eturned home, they hoped that evelopments during the war would

The women of the 6888ᵗʰ worked seven days a week in eight-hour rotating shifts to deal with the volume of mail for soldiers in Europe.

bring them equality. However, they saw that little had changed.

On July 26, 1948, President Harry Truman issued Executive Order 9981, stating that there should be equal treatment and opportunity for all persons in the armed services. Finally, at least on paper, the military would be fully integrated.

The Delayed Medals of Honor

When World War II ended, no African American had been awarded the Medal of Honor. In 1993, the Army had a team look into the matter, and a number of African Americans were recommended for the award. In January 1997, seven African American World War II soldiers were finally awarded the Medal of Honor. Only one was still living and able to receive his award in person.

The 1950s and 1960s

The 1950s were a time of change for the military. In 1950, integration of the military was taking place very slowly. Despite Executive Order 9981, the U.S. military was still largely segregated, especially the Army and the Navy. The Defense Department realized that because of racial prejudice, African Americans in the military were not being used fully. This led to new opportunities for African Americans.

The Korean War

In June 1950, troops from North Korea invaded South Korea. The United States sent combat forces to support South Korea. In August 1950, the Army training center in Fort Jackson, South Carolina, began receiving recruits for the war. The commander tried to have separate training groups for people of different races, but there were so many recruits that this was not practical. Soon, the commander ended segregated training. Training went so well at Fort Jackson that, by the end of 1950, all of the Army's basic training centers had been successfully integrated.

In October 1951, the Army **disbanded** the 24th Regiment, an African American unit that had existed since 1869. For all practical purposes, this ended segregation in the Army. By the time the Korean War ended in 1953, the U.S. military had been changed forever. For the first time, people of different races served together in the same units, and African Americans were given the same opportunity to lead in combat.

By the 1950s, African Americans were in command of integrated units.

Civil Rights

In the 1950s and early 1960s, African Americans were still battling discrimination and segregation in many places in the United States, especially the South. The civil rights movement began, with African American leaders such as Martin Luther King Jr. organizing marches and other nonviolent protests to demand equal rights.

The military, previously known for its segregation, was now one of the most integrated institutions in the country. New recruits of all races trained together, lived in the same barracks, and ate in the same halls. Young African American men thought they might have better opportunities for good jobs and advancement in the military than they would in other parts of U.S. society, where African Americans were struggling for their rights. African Americans had never seen a better time to enlist.

Daniel "Chappie" James Jr. became the first African American to command an integrated fighter squadron in July 1951.

The Vietnam War

Quick Facts

In 1965, African Americans made up 15 percent of the U.S. Army, 5 percent of the Navy, 9 percent of the Marines, and 8 percent of the Air Force.

The Vietnam War was a conflict in Southeast Asia. On one side there was Communist North Vietnam, supported by such countries as China and the Soviet Union. On the other side, non-Communist South Vietnam was supported by non-Communist countries such as the United States. When North Vietnam sought to take over South Vietnam, a long war developed. At first, in the 1950s and early 1960s, the United States sent only military advisers and supplies. By the late 1960s, however, more than 500,000 U.S. troops had been sent to Vietnam.

A Difficult War

Vietnam was a difficult war, and many Americans were opposed to involvement in the conflict. In addition, many African Americans felt that they were bearing too large share of the military burden. African Americans represented 9.3 percent of all U.S. armed forces, but they made up 15 percent of those serving in Vietnam. They were more often assigned to combat duty and made up of a disproportionately large share of casualties. Young African American men were also drafted at a higher rate than other men. In 1968 for example, 64 percent of eligible African Americans were drafted, compared with only 31 percent of eligible men of other races.

Soldiers in Vietnam faced difficulties fighting in hot, humid jungles.

In 1973, a peace agreement was reached, and U.S. troops withdrew from Vietnam. During the war, almost 275,000 African Americans served in the U.S. armed forces, making up 9.8 percent of all troops. Of these, 7,243 died in combat. Twenty African Americans were awarded the Medal of Honor for their service in Vietnam.

A life-size statue of three soldiers of different races stands at the Vietnam Veterans Memorial in Washington, D.C.

Fred Cherry

Colonel Fred Cherry was born in 1928 in Virginia. He became an Air Force pilot, flying bombing missions over North Vietnam. In October 1965, he was shot down and became the first African American pilot captured in North Vietnam. Cherry had numerous injuries, including a wounded shoulder that required surgery. He did not receive the proper treatment and suffered serious complications as a result. He was also tortured by his captors. Cherry was finally freed when the war ended in 1973. He received numerous awards, including the Air Force Cross and two Purple Hearts.

The Gulf Wars and Afghanistan

The events leading to the first Persian Gulf War, often called Operation Desert Storm, began in 1990 when Iraq, led by its dictator, Saddam Hussein, invaded Kuwait. In response, a multinational **coalition** force, led by the United States, bombed Iraq beginning in January 1991 and sent ground troops into Iraq the next month. Unlike the Vietnam War, which went on for years, Operation Desert Storm ended quickly, with few U.S. casualties.

The position of African Americans during the first Persian Gulf War had changed, compared with previous wars. Since the U.S. military draft had ended in the 1970s, the armed forces were made up completely of volunteers. There were proportionately more African Americans in the armed forces than in the overall U.S. population. They made up more than 20 percent of U.S. troops. In addition, of all U.S. women who enlisted, 48 percent were African American. There were also more African Americans in leadership positions than ever before, most notably General Colin Powell.

More than 500,000 U.S. troops were sent to fight in the first Persian Gulf War, which began in January 1991.

Afghanistan and the Second Gulf War

U.S. forces were again involved in the Persian Gulf area beginning in late 2001, following the September 11 terrorist attacks on the World Trade Center in New York and the Pentagon outside Washington, D.C. In October, in Operation Enduring Freedom, the United States and Great Britain launched air strikes on Afghanistan, targeting the terrorist organization al-Qaeda and the Taliban militia. While U.S. troops were actively engaged in Afghanistan, the Iraq war, often called the Second Gulf War, began in March 2003. President George W. Bush, who believed that Iraq was producing destructive weapons, ordered an invasion of that country.

Both wars were long and difficult. In the Iraq War alone, more than 4,000 Americans were killed and more than 36,000 wounded. Some 9 percent of the deaths were among African Americans. Many Americans were opposed to both wars while at the same time supporting the troops who fought. Although thousands of African Americans served in both wars, support for the efforts among African Americans was also mixed. In addition, in large part because of opposition to the Iraq and Afghanistan wars, enlistment levels among African Americans dropped significantly. African Americans made up 20 percent of active-duty recruits in 2000, but the figure dropped to 13 percent in 2006.

Colin Powell

Colin Powell was born in New York City in 1937. While he was in college, he joined **ROTC**, the Reserve Officers' Training Corps. After graduation, he joined the Army and in 1962 was sent to Vietnam as a military adviser. Powell served two tours of combat duty in Vietnam, earning a Purple Heart and a Bronze Star. He was regularly promoted and filled a number of roles. In 1987, he became the first African American national security adviser, and in 1989, he became the first African American chairman of the Joint Chiefs of Staff. Powell was responsible for overseeing all U.S. military operations during the Gulf War and became familiar to the public during news conferences and press briefings. It was the first time that most Americans had seen an African American military leader in a position of such authority. In 1993, Powell retired from the military with the rank of four-star general. In 2001, President George W. Bush appointed him Secretary of State, a position he held for four years.

Recent Developments

Today, the U.S. military is very diverse racially. As of 2008, 16.7 percent of military personnel were African American. At the time, African Americans made up 13.5 percent of the U.S. population, so they were represented at a higher level in the military. African Americans made up 22.7 percent of the Army, 21.3 percent of the Navy, 17.8 percent of the Air Force, and 11.6 percent of the Marine Corps. African Americans made up only 8 percent of senior military officers, while people of European heritage made up 77 percent of senior officers.

In 2007, the Military Leadership Diversity Commission was formed to examine and promote policies that provide leadership opportunities for minorities in the armed forces.

That same year, the Army Chief of Staff, General George W. Casey Jr., announced the creation of a Diversity Task Force. The task force was created to increase awareness about racial issues within the military and develop ways to increase diversity. Casey stated, "I will tell you that I firmly believe the strength of our Army comes from our diversity."

Brigadier General Belinda Pinckney, an African American woman, was appointed as the first head of the task force.

African American troops have played an integral role in recent conflicts, including Iraq and Afghanistan.

African American Women in the Military

Through much of history, war has been seen as a man's domain. However, women, including African American women, have sought to serve in the U.S. military for many years. African American women may well have served in some capacity during the American Revolution, taking care of the wounded or even disguising themselves as men so they could fight. During the Civil War, African American women worked alongside women of European heritage, performing nursing chores, cooking for soldiers, and laundering their uniforms. During World War I, many trained African American nurses were turned down when they tried to join the Army or Navy Nurse Corps. Finally, after the war ended, 18 African American nurses were allowed into the Army Nurse Corps. They lived in segregated barracks and cared only for African American soldiers or prisoners of war.

Many African American women served as nurses during World War II. In addition, 4,000 African American women enlisted in the WACs and 60 in the Navy WAVES, or Women Accepted for Volunteer Emergency Service. In 1948, President Harry Truman signed into law a measure permitting women in the Army and the **Reserves**. From this point on, women of all races were allowed to participate more fully in the military. In September 1979, Hazel Winifred Johnson became the first African American woman general in the U.S. Army when she was promoted to chief of the Army Nurse Corps. Today, about half of all the women in the U.S. armed forces are African American.

Timeline

1775–1783: Colonists fight for their independence from Great Britain in the American Revolution. At first, African Americans are not permitted to fight, but up to 10,000 eventually are involved on the colonial side.

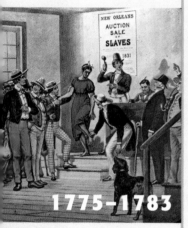

1775–1783

1792: The U.S. Congress passes a law saying that only men of European heritage can serve in the military.

1812–1815

1812–1815: African Americans join the War of 1812, after Congress passes a law allowing the enlistment of "persons of color."

1814: A U.S. War Department memo describes African Americans as "unfit to associate with the American soldier."

1815: Congress passes a measure providing for an army of 10,000 men, but no African Americans are recruited.

1820s: African Americans are prohibited from serving in the U.S. Army or state militias.

1830s: The U.S. Navy imposes a quota to limit the number of African American sailors to less than 5 percent of the total.

1861: Abraham Lincoln becomes president, and the Civil War begins between the North and South. Slavery is one of the main issues. At first, Lincoln is reluctant to allow the enlistment of African Americans, but regiments of African American volunteers are formed.

1863: As a result of the Emancipation Proclamation, former slaves and other African Americans serve in the Union military.

1863

1865: The Civil War ends. With the passage of the Thirteenth Amendment, slavery is abolished.

1866: Congress passes a law allowing African Americans to serve in the regular peacetime Army. African American Army regiments are created.

1867: The Buffalo Soldiers are sent to the West to fight in the Indian wars.

1877: Henry O. Flipper becomes the first African American to graduate from the U.S. Military Academy at West Point.

1898: African American soldiers take part in some of the key battles fought during the Spanish-American War.

1917–1918: The United States fights in World War I. Many African Americans line up to enlist, and the government creates two new African American combat units.

1700   **1800**   **1850**   **1900**

1940: While World War II is being fought in Europe, the United States enacts its first peacetime military draft. Many African Americans are turned down when they try to register.

1941–1945: The United States fights in World War II. President Franklin D. Roosevelt signs an executive order barring discrimination in the defense industry.

1941: Benjamin O. Davis Sr. becomes the first African American brigadier general.

1942: Dorie Miller becomes the first African American to receive the Navy Cross for his actions at Pearl Harbor.

1943: The Tuskegee Airmen are sent to fight in World War II.

1948: President Harry Truman issues Executive Order 9981, directing the integration of the U.S. military.

1950–1953: The United States sends troops to fight in the Korean War. During the course of the war, segregation ends in the Army.

1953: Benjamin O. Davis Jr. becomes the first African American Air Force officer to become a general.

1965–1973: U.S. troops are actively involved in the Vietnam War. African Americans make up 15 percent of combat troops.

1973: The military draft ends, and the United States begins having all-volunteer forces.

1979: Hazel Winifred Johnson becomes the first African American woman general in the U.S. Army.

1987: Colin Powell becomes the first African American national security adviser.

1989: Colin Powell becomes the first African American chairman of the Joint Chiefs of Staff.

1991: Colin Powell oversees all U.S. operations in the first Gulf War.

1997: Seven African American soldiers, only one of whom is alive, are awarded the Medal of Honor for service during World War II.

2001: In Operation Enduring Freedom, air strikes are launched on Afghanistan in October 2001. Troops, including African Americans, are sent to the region.

2003: African Americans are among the thousands of U.S. troops sent to Iraq in the Second Gulf War.

2007: The Military Leadership Diversity Commission and the Diversity Task Force are created to examine policies on diversity within the military and increase awareness of racial issues.

1940   **1960**   **1980**   **2000**

Activity

Be an Ambassador of Equality

Prejudice occurs when you make a judgment about someone without getting to know that person. Sometimes, these judgments are based on skin color, but prejudice can also be based on culture, gender, religion, or even age.

You will need:

✓ a pen
✓ paper

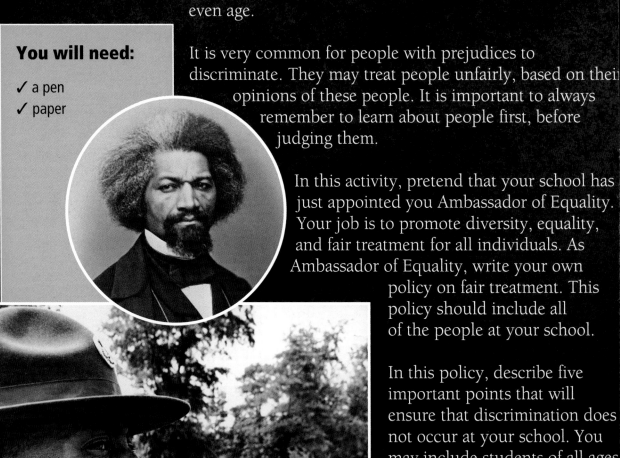

It is very common for people with prejudices to discriminate. They may treat people unfairly, based on their opinions of these people. It is important to always remember to learn about people first, before judging them.

In this activity, pretend that your school has just appointed you Ambassador of Equality. Your job is to promote diversity, equality, and fair treatment for all individuals. As Ambassador of Equality, write your own policy on fair treatment. This policy should include all of the people at your school.

In this policy, describe five important points that will ensure that discrimination does not occur at your school. You may include students of all ages. Don't forget the teachers!

Tips: What rights do all students have? Do they differ from the rights of teachers?

Q When did the American Revolution take place?

A 1775 to 1783

Q Who were the Tuskegee Airmen?

A The Tuskegee Airmen were the first African American combat pilots. They fought in World War II.

Q Who was the first African American Air Force officer to become a general?

Q Who were the Buffalo Soldiers?

A The Buffalo Soldiers were regiments of African American soldiers who fought in the Indian wars.

A Benjamin O. Davis Jr.

Q What is the Medal of Honor?

A The Medal of Honor is the highest decoration a U.S. soldier can be awarded. It is given for service above and beyond the call of duty.

Q Who was Henry O. Flipper?

A Henry O. Flipper was the first African American to graduate from the U.S. Military Academy at West Point, in 1877.

Q What was the Executive Order 9981?

A This order, issued by President Harry Truman in 1948, said that all people in the armed forces were to be treated equally.

Glossary

abolitionist movement: a movement to end slavery

cavalry: soldiers fighting on horseback

chaplains: people who conduct religious services for the military

coalition: a temporary union between groups

Continental Army: the army formed by the colonists after the American Revolution began

desertion: leaving the military before one's tour of duty is up

disbanded: broken up and dismissed from service

discrimination: unfair treatment because of a person's race, gender, age, or physical or mental condition

eloquent: using beautiful and powerful language

Emancipation Proclamation: an order issued during the Civil War by President Lincoln to free the slaves living in the Confederacy

embezzlement: stealing money or assets from some other person or group

enlist: to join the military

exempt: free from a duty or obligation

inaugurated: formally inducted into office

industrialization: the move from an economy that depends on agriculture to one that depends on the production of goods

infantry: soldiers fighting on foot

integrated: open to all people, no matter what their race, gender, or religion

Medal of Honor: the highest military honor in the United States, given by Congress for acts of bravery in times of danger

militias: armies composed of ordinary citizens who volunteer on a temporary basis

mortally wounded: injured so badly that death occurs

neutral: not taking a side in a dispute

pensions: money given to people on a regular basis after they have performed some type of service

posthumously: after someone's death

prejudice: a hatred, fear, or mistrust of someone because of his or her race, religion, or nationality

quota: a maximum number that is permitted

recruited: enlisted for a military group

regiment: a permanent milit unit of soldiers, usually mad up of two or three battalions of ground troops divided int smaller companies

Reserves: part of a country's military forces, consisting of people who are not on active duty but are called upon during emergencies

ROTC: Reserve Officers' Training Corps, a program in which college students undergo military training to become officers

segregated: having separate facilities for people of differe races, genders, or religions

smoke jumpers: firefighters who parachute into remote areas to extinguish forest fire

surveyor: someone who takes accurate measurements of land areas in order to determine boundaries

Index

Log on to www.av2books.com

AV² by Weigl brings you media enhanced books that support active learning. Go to www.av2books.com, and enter the special code found on page 2 of this book. You will gain access to enriched and enhanced content that supplements and complements this book. Content includes video, audio, web links, quizzes, a slide show, and activities.

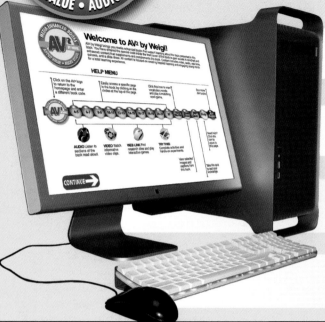

Audio
Listen to sections of
the book read aloud.

Video
Watch informative video clips.

Embedded Weblinks
Gain additional information
for research.

Try This!
Complete activities and
hands-on experiments.

WHAT'S ONLINE?

Try This!	Embedded Weblinks	Video	EXTRA FEATURES
Test your knowledge of important events in African American military history.	Find out more about the history of African Americans in the military.	Watch a video about African Americans in the military.	**Audio** Listen to sections of the book read aloud.
Write a biography about a notable African American who served in the military.	Learn more about notable people from **Great African Americans–Military**.	Watch a video about a notable moment of African Americans in the military.	**Key Words** Study vocabulary, and complete a matching word activity.
Create a timeline of important events in an African American military person's life.	Link to more notable achievements of African Americans in the military.		**Slide Show** View images and captio and prepare a presentat
Complete a writing activity about an important topic in the book.			**Quizzes** Test your knowledge.
Design your own memorial for African Americans who served in the military.			

AV² was built to bridge the gap between print and digital. We encourage you to tell us what you like and what you want to see in the future.

Sign up to be an AV² Ambassador at www.av2books.com/ambassador.